Being Different

Yani Dernedde

Presentation by *BookLeaf Publishing*

Web: www.bookleafpub.com

E-mail: info@bookleafpub.com

ISBN: 9789357445436

First edition 2022

DEDICATION

To my children

'I love you with all my heart'

PREFACE

It's not easy to be different than others. I refer to anything which doesn't fit the mainstream: opinions, physical disability, clothes, colour, accent and nationalities. Nevertheless, I think it is important not to lose yourself in the middle of similarity. Being different actually contributes to make the world a better place. Can you imagine the world without variety?
Embrace your uniqueness.

The Label

you are very organised
you have boxes for everything
you always label your boxes
"it's easier for a search," you said

you put me in a box too
but isn't sure
what kind of sort
"human, you should label me a HUMAN," I said

Bring Me Back to My Childhood

bring me back to my childhood
where worries couldn't be understood
tomorrow could wait
and time was refused to be set

where honesty was not impolite
no matter what
at the end was always lights

where my friends would never say but
my mouth would never be shut
my colour didn't make anyone enraged
and my smile would never be faked

where we didn't care
about the name of a place we lived
the language we were supposed to speak
the clothes we wore so we could fit.

Different

I might speak a different accent
wear a different pigment
was born in a different continent
but it DOESN'T mean
I'm a less human.

Action

I do not accept
I do not expect
But I do act

Unique

I will not laugh at you
because you're all the same
but don't judge me
because I'm different

Your Solid Mind

In your solid mind, I'm far out
So you said, stay out
Then I shouted the standard out
You let me in
But not into your mind

In your solid mind, I'm far out
Because I have a different tongue and it
produces a different sound
Calamitous, disastrous, the end of the world, you
said
Then you shouted the standard out
And I'm far out

I'm still in and still human
Invisible, each time, each sitting
Not worth to be heard of

In your solid mind, I'm far out
My words were just sound
Backfired, faster than a hound
No one could help because all friends were out
of bounds

In your solid mind, I'm far out

I couldn't reach nor breach your mind
You said, you're sorry
I wished that had come from your mind

In your solid mind, I'm far out
I'm not the standard, so please go out

Not Again

you
underestimated
me
again and again

I
always forgave
you
but not again

hope - a haiku

waves of fire hit me
rain rinsed and washed my scorched skin
ignites hope within

Hellfire

I'll walk you through the hellfire
where I'll burn your monstrous desire
where your scream will go higher and higher
then you'll clench your fist tighter
calling me a fucking liar
and I'll make sure
you'll hear
my delighted laughter

Un-friends

yes, I called you friends
but that's before you left me in the rain
almost drown in the deep murky puddle
I cried for help
you turned your back and closed your eyes
terrible watchers indeed
I wonder
why did you so afraid to speak up?
think of how many lives would have been saved
if you had spoken your hearts out
no, I will not call you friends

The Peculiar Dominants

at the beginning
you cheered
halfway
you sheared
at the end
you buried

too bad
I'm not dead
not yet

I'll replace
the flag you raised
with tons of ice

The Scars

she cannot endure
the inflicted scars
cannot be obscured
not anymore

so, she wears them proudly
they should remind her
of the mistake she has made
trusting them

Breathing

I just need to stop
and breathe
I feel your claws
pierce my skin
breathe
I see blood
drip drip drip
keep breathing
I see you walk away
with a smile
on your lips
I'm out of breath

Pity

I'm not angry with you
in fact
I pity you

who wears beautiful jargon
stuck on your forehead
instead of living it

who wears a bargain
and breeds hatred
waiting to hit

who beholds me as a burden
as a target
digging the darkest pit

no, I'm not angry with you
but I don't stand and watch either
how you're treating others

I take action
declare NO to your selection
NO to being silenced

now I put you in a place

not to judge the human race
based only on the face

cheers to human kind
of any kind
peace at last in my mind

no, I'm not angry with you
I have forgiven you
in fact, I pity you

Not me

your sweet lullaby soothes everyone
except me

I wish

I wish
I didn't except
your invitation

I wish
I didn't believe in
your institution

I wish
I knew your smile wasn't just
an animation

I wish
I could escape
your isolation

Proud

I'm different
I'm proud of it

a new start - a haiku

walking through sunshine
warming my skin and my heart
hope for a new start

never giving up

I remember those fucking faces
as fresh as morning dew
full of hate and underestimated
that's why
I will never give up

home

home is
where I feel accepted
where I feel trusted
where I can be myself
where my opinion counts
where my freedom is not just a sound

Each

every.
each.
of.
you.
is.
equal.

www.ingramcontent.com/pod-product-compliance
Lightning Source LLC
LaVergne TN
LVHW021357200726
843509LV00014B/2897